LAKELAND TERRIER

INTRODUCTION TO THE BREED

The Lakeland Terrier is a small to medium-sized breed known for its spunky personality, striking appearance, and versatility. This breed is highly regarded for its intelligence, agility, and courage, making it a popular choice among dog enthusiasts worldwide. Lakeland Terriers are not only cherished companions but also skilled hunters and show dogs.

ORIGINS AND HISTORY

Originally hailing from the Lake District in England, the Lakeland Terrier has a rich history dating back to the 19th century. It was developed to assist farmers in controlling vermin populations, particularly foxes and badgers, that posed a threat to livestock. The breed's exact origins are unclear, but it is believed to be a result of crossing several terrier breeds, including the Bedlington Terrier and the Border Terrier.

The Lakeland Terrier's distinctive appearance and working ability gained recognition in the early 20th century. In 1921, the breed was officially recognized by The Kennel Club in the United Kingdom. Shortly after, it started gaining popularity in various dog *shows for its unique look and impressive capabilities in the field.*

Over the years, the Lakeland Terrier's role as a hunting dog diminished, but its popularity as a companion and show dog soared. It gradually transitioned from being solely a working breed to a well-rounded family pet, known for its cheerful disposition and loyalty.

Today, the Lakeland Terrier is cherished by dog enthusiasts around the world. It continues to thrive in various canine activities, including conformation shows, obedience trials, and agility competitions. Its tenacious spirit and lively personality make it an ideal companion for active individuals or families seeking a spirited and devoted canine partner.

LAKELAND TERRIER

PHYSICAL CHARACTERISTICS

The Lakeland Terrier is a small to medium-sized breed with a sturdy and well-proportioned body. Here are some notable physical characteristics:

- *SIZE:*

  Lakeland Terriers typically stand between 13.5 and 15.5 inches (34-39 cm) at the shoulder.

- *WEIGHT:*

  The breed generally weighs between 15 and 17 pounds (7-8 kg).

- *COAT:*

  The Lakeland Terrier has a dense, wiry, and weather-resistant double coat. The outer coat is harsh and straight, while the undercoat is soft and dense.

- *COLOR:*

  The breed comes in various colors, including black, blue, liver, red, wheaten, or combinations of these colors.

- *HEAD:*

  Lakeland Terriers have a moderately broad head with a defined stop. The eyes are dark and alert, and the ears are small, V-shaped, and fold forward.

- *BODY:*

  Their body is compact, with a level topline and a deep chest. The tail is docked to a medium length and carried upright.

UNIQUE FEATURES

In addition to its physical characteristics, the Lakeland Terrier possesses several unique features that distinguish it from other breeds:

- *EXPRESSION:*

  The Lakeland Terrier has a keen and intelligent expression, reflecting its alert and inquisitive nature.

- *HAND-STRIPPING:*

  Unlike many other breeds, the Lakeland Terrier's coat does not shed much. It requires hand-stripping, a process of removing dead hair by hand, to maintain its texture and appearance.

- *BEARD AND EYEBROWS:*

  This breed is known for its distinctive facial furnishings, including a beard and bushy eyebrows, which enhance its charming and expressive appearance.

- *VERSATILITY:*

  Despite its small size, the Lakeland Terrier is a versatile dog. It excels in various activities, including obedience, agility, tracking, and earthdog trials, showcasing its adaptability and intelligence.

- *FEARLESSNESS:*

  Lakeland Terriers are courageous and fearless. Their bold nature, combined with their size and agility, makes them confident and capable companions.

The physical characteristics and unique features of the Lakeland Terrier contribute to its distinct charm and appeal, both in the show ring and as a beloved family pet.

LAKELAND TERRIER

UNIQUE FEATURES

The Lakeland Terrier possesses several distinctive features that make it stand out among other breeds:

- *HAND-STRIPPING:*

  Unlike many other breeds, the Lakeland Terrier's coat does not shed much. It requires hand-stripping, a process of removing dead hair by hand, to maintain its texture and appearance.

- *EXPRESSION:*

  The Lakeland Terrier has a keen and intelligent expression, reflecting its alert and inquisitive nature.

- *FACIAL FURNISHINGS:*

  This breed is known for its distinctive facial furnishings, including a beard and bushy eyebrows, which enhance its charming and expressive appearance.

- *VERSATILITY:*

  Despite its small size, the Lakeland Terrier is a versatile dog. It excels in various activities, including obedience, agility, tracking, and earthdog trials, showcasing its adaptability and intelligence.

- *FEARLESSNESS:*

    Lakeland Terriers are courageous and fearless. Their bold nature, combined with their size and agility, makes them confident and capable companions.

The unique features of the Lakeland Terrier contribute to its distinct charm and appeal, both in the show ring and as a beloved family pet.

LAKELAND TERRIER

DIFFERENT COLOR VARIATIONS

The Lakeland Terrier comes in various color variations, adding to its visual appeal. Here are some common colors found in this breed:

- *BLACK:*

  Lakeland Terriers can have a solid black coat, which gives them a striking and sleek appearance.

- *BLUE:*

  The breed also comes in a beautiful blue color, ranging from a dark steel blue to a lighter shade.

- *LIVER:*

  Some Lakeland Terriers have a liver-colored coat, which can vary from a deep reddish-brown to a lighter tan color.

- *RED:*

  Another color variation is red, which can range from a vibrant, deep red to a lighter, golden hue.

- *WHEATEN:*

  Wheaten is a popular color in Lakeland Terriers. It is a pale, warm shade of beige or tan, resembling the color of ripened wheat.

- *COMBINATIONS:*

  Additionally, there can be various combinations of these colors. For example, a Lakeland Terrier might have a wheaten base coat with black or blue markings.

The different color variations of the Lakeland Terrier allow for individuality and make each dog unique. Regardless of the color, all Lakeland Terriers share the same spirited and lovable temperament.

LAKELAND TERRIER

TEMPERAMENT AND PERSONALITY TRAITS

The Lakeland Terrier is known for its distinctive temperament and unique personality traits, making it a delightful companion. Here are some key characteristics of this breed:

- *FEARLESS:*

  Lakeland Terriers are bold and fearless dogs. Despite their small size, they possess a courageous spirit and are not easily intimidated.

- *INTELLIGENT:*

  This breed is highly intelligent and quick to learn. They thrive on mental stimulation and enjoy engaging in problem-solving activities.

- *INDEPENDENT:*

  Lakeland Terriers have an independent streak and can exhibit a self-reliant nature. They are known to make their own decisions and can be somewhat stubborn at times.

- *ALERT:*

With their keen senses, Lakeland Terriers are highly alert and make excellent watchdogs. They will readily alert their owners to any potential dangers or strangers approaching.

- *PLAYFUL:*

Despite their serious side, Lakeland Terriers have a playful and lively nature. They enjoy interactive playtime and appreciate activities that keep them mentally and physically stimulated.

- *LOYAL:*

This breed forms strong bonds with their families and is known for their unwavering loyalty. They thrive on companionship and enjoy being involved in their owners' daily lives.

- *CONFIDENT:*

Lakeland Terriers exude confidence in their demeanor. They carry themselves with a self-assured and determined attitude.

The temperament and personality traits of the Lakeland Terrier contribute to its overall charm and make it an engaging and devoted companion for those who appreciate its spirited nature.

LAKELAND TERRIER

SOCIALIZING WITH HUMANS

The Lakeland Terrier is a sociable breed that generally enjoys being around humans. Here are some key points regarding their socialization with humans:

- *FRIENDLY:*

  Lakeland Terriers are known for their friendly nature and generally get along well with people. They are often affectionate towards their family members and enjoy spending time with them.

- *GOOD WITH CHILDREN:*

  When properly socialized and raised with children, Lakeland Terriers can be excellent companions for kids. They have a playful and energetic nature that can make them great playmates.

- *INTERACTION:*

  This breed appreciates social interaction with humans and thrives on attention and positive reinforcement. Regular playtime, training sessions, and bonding activities help strengthen the bond between the dog and its human family members.

- *ALERTNESS:*

  Lakeland Terriers are naturally alert, which makes
  them capable watchdogs. They may exhibit protective
  instincts towards their families, alerting them to
  potential dangers or strangers approaching the home.

SOCIALIZING WITH OTHER ANIMALS

*Socializing a Lakeland Terrier with other animals is
important to ensure positive and harmonious
interactions. Here are some considerations:*

- *EARLY SOCIALIZATION:*

  Starting early is crucial in introducing a Lakeland
  Terrier to other animals. Proper socialization during
  their formative weeks and months can help them
  develop good manners and positive associations with
  other pets.

- *SUPERVISION:*

  When introducing a Lakeland Terrier to other animals,
  supervision is necessary, especially during the initial
  interactions. This helps prevent any potential conflicts
  and allows for a controlled introduction.

- *POSITIVE REINFORCEMENT:*

Reward-based training methods and positive reinforcement can encourage desirable behavior and help the Lakeland Terrier associate positive experiences with other animals.

- *INDIVIDUAL PERSONALITY:*

Each Lakeland Terrier may have a unique personality and tolerance level towards other animals. Some may get along well with other dogs or cats, while others may be more selective. It is important to consider the individual temperament and preferences of the dog when introducing them to new animal companions.

With proper socialization, the Lakeland Terrier can learn to coexist peacefully with humans and other animals, fostering positive relationships and a harmonious household.

LAKELAND TERRIER

POPULARITY AS PETS

The Lakeland Terrier is a breed that has gained popularity as a pet for various reasons. Here are some factors contributing to its appeal:

- *ADAPTABILITY:*

    Lakeland Terriers can adapt well to different living situations, making them suitable for both apartments and houses. Their size and energy levels can be well managed in various environments.

- *SIZE:*

    Being a small to medium-sized breed, Lakeland Terriers are a popular choice for those seeking a compact yet sturdy companion. Their size makes them suitable for families with limited space or individuals looking for a manageable-sized dog.

- *VERSATILITY:*

    The Lakeland Terrier's versatility is another reason for its popularity. They excel in various activities, including obedience, agility, and tracking. This makes them appealing to individuals who enjoy participating in canine sports and activities.

- *PLAYFULNESS:*

  Lakeland Terriers have a playful and energetic nature. Their love for interactive playtime can be entertaining for families and individuals who enjoy an active lifestyle.

- *LOYAL COMPANIONSHIP:*

  This breed forms strong bonds with their owners and is known for their loyalty. They thrive on companionship and enjoy being part of their human family's daily activities.

- *DISTINCTIVE APPEARANCE:*

  The Lakeland Terrier's unique appearance, including its wiry coat and expressive face, contributes to its appeal as a pet. Many people are drawn to its charming and distinctive appearance.

- *TRAINABILITY:*

  Lakeland Terriers are intelligent and quick to learn, making them trainable. Their willingness to please their owners and their ability to grasp commands and tasks make them enjoyable to train.

Due to these qualities, the Lakeland Terrier has garnered a significant following and continues to be a popular choice for individuals and families seeking a spirited, versatile, and devoted companion.

LAKELAND TERRIER

ROLE IN THERAPY AND EMOTIONAL SUPPORT WORK

The Lakeland Terrier can play a valuable role in therapy and emotional support work, providing comfort, companionship, and emotional support to individuals in need. Here are some aspects of their role in these areas:

- *EMOTIONAL SUPPORT:*

  Lakeland Terriers are known for their ability to form deep emotional connections with their owners. Their affectionate and loyal nature can bring comfort and emotional support to individuals experiencing anxiety, stress, or emotional challenges.

- *COMPANION ANIMALS:*

  These dogs can serve as wonderful companion animals for individuals with mental health conditions or those going through therapy. Their presence and unwavering companionship can help alleviate feelings of loneliness and provide a sense of security.

- *THERAPEUTIC VISITS:*

Lakeland Terriers can participate in therapy animal programs where they visit hospitals, nursing homes, and other facilities. During these visits, they provide comfort and joy to patients, residents, and staff, promoting positive emotional well-being.

- *CALMING INFLUENCE:*

The calm and soothing demeanor of Lakeland Terriers can have a positive impact on individuals experiencing stress, anxiety, or PTSD. Their presence can help reduce anxiety levels and provide a source of comfort and stability.

- *NON-JUDGMENTAL SUPPORT:*

These dogs offer non-judgmental support, allowing individuals to express themselves freely and without fear of criticism. They create a safe space where individuals can relax, share their thoughts, and receive unconditional love and acceptance.

The affectionate and understanding nature of Lakeland Terriers makes them well-suited for therapy and emotional support work, helping to enhance the overall well-being and quality of life of those they interact with.

CHALLENGES OF OWNING THIS BREED

While owning a Lakeland Terrier can be a rewarding experience, it also comes with certain challenges that potential owners should be aware of:

- *HIGH ENERGY:*

  Lakeland Terriers are an active and energetic breed that requires regular exercise and mental stimulation. Meeting their exercise needs can be a challenge for individuals with busy schedules or those unable to provide sufficient physical activity.

- *GROOMING DEMANDS:*

  The wiry double coat of Lakeland Terriers requires regular grooming and hand-stripping to maintain its texture and appearance. This grooming process can be time-consuming and may require professional assistance or learning the techniques yourself.

- *INDEPENDENT NATURE:*

  Lakeland Terriers have an independent streak and can exhibit stubbornness. Training and consistent positive reinforcement are necessary to overcome these traits and ensure proper obedience and behavior.

- *STRONG PREY DRIVE:*

  Due to their hunting background, Lakeland Terriers may have a strong prey drive. This can make them prone to chasing small animals, so careful supervision and appropriate training are necessary to manage this instinctual behavior.

- *SOCIALIZATION NEEDS:*

  Proper socialization is essential for Lakeland Terriers to ensure they get along well with other dogs and animals. This process may require time and effort to expose them to different environments, people, and pets.

REWARDS OF OWNING THIS BREED

Despite the challenges, owning a Lakeland Terrier can be highly rewarding and fulfilling for the right owner. Some of the rewards of owning this breed include:

- *LIVELY AND SPIRITED COMPANION:*

  Lakeland Terriers are full of energy and possess a lively and spirited personality. Their playful nature and enthusiastic spirit can bring joy and entertainment to their owners.

- *LOYAL AND DEVOTED:*

These dogs form strong bonds with their owners and are known for their unwavering loyalty. They are dedicated companions who thrive on the love and attention they receive from their human family members.

- ## *VERSATILE AND INTELLIGENT:*

Lakeland Terriers are highly intelligent and versatile. Their intelligence makes them quick learners and enables them to excel in various activities, such as obedience, agility, and tracking.

- ## *PROTECTIVE NATURE:*

Lakeland Terriers have a protective instinct towards their families. Their alertness and courage make them excellent watchdogs, providing a sense of security for their owners.

- ## *BONDING OPPORTUNITIES:*

Through training, socialization, and interactive playtime, owners have the opportunity to develop a strong bond with their Lakeland Terrier. The mutual trust and companionship that can be built with this breed can be incredibly rewarding.

With proper care, training, and attention, the challenges can be overcome, and the rewards of owning a Lakeland Terrier can make for a fulfilling and joyful companionship.

LAKELAND TERRIER

LAKELAND TERRIER AND CHILDREN

The Lakeland Terrier can have a harmonious relationship with children when proper interactions and guidelines are followed. Here are some tips for fostering a positive and safe relationship between a Lakeland Terrier and children:

- *SUPERVISION:*

  It is crucial to supervise interactions between the Lakeland Terrier and children, especially younger ones. This ensures the safety of both the dog and the child and allows for immediate intervention if necessary.

- *TEACH GENTLE TOUCH:*

  Teach children to interact gently with the Lakeland Terrier, avoiding rough play or pulling on the dog's ears or tail. Encourage them to approach the dog calmly and to pet them gently.

- *EDUCATE CHILDREN ABOUT BOUNDARIES:*

  Teach children to respect the Lakeland Terrier's personal space and provide them with guidelines on appropriate behavior around the dog. This includes not bothering the dog while they are eating or sleeping.

- *SOCIALIZE EARLY:*

Properly socialize the Lakeland Terrier with children from a young age. Expose them to positive experiences with children, gradually increasing their exposure and ensuring they have pleasant interactions.

- *TEACH PROPER HANDLING:*

Educate children on how to handle the Lakeland Terrier gently and properly. Teach them to support the dog's body when picking them up and to avoid actions that may cause discomfort or distress.

- *POSITIVE REINFORCEMENT:*

Encourage children to engage in positive interactions with the Lakeland Terrier and reward them for respectful behavior towards the dog. This helps establish a positive association and reinforces appropriate conduct.

- *SET BOUNDARIES FOR THE DOG:*

Establish boundaries for the Lakeland Terrier, such as creating designated safe spaces where the dog can retreat when they need a break from interactions with children. Teach children to respect these boundaries.

By following these tips and providing guidance, children can develop a respectful and harmonious relationship with the Lakeland Terrier, fostering a positive and safe environment for both the dog and the children.

LAKELAND TERRIER

COMMON BEHAVIORAL ISSUES

Like any breed, Lakeland Terriers may experience certain behavioral issues. Here are some common behavioral issues that can arise in this breed:

- *EXCESSIVE BARKING:*

  Lakeland Terriers are known for their vocal nature and may be prone to excessive barking. This can occur when they are bored, anxious, or trying to communicate something. Consistent training and providing mental and physical stimulation can help address this behavior.

- *SEPARATION ANXIETY:*

  Some Lakeland Terriers may develop separation anxiety, experiencing distress when left alone. This can lead to destructive behavior, excessive barking, or house soiling. Gradual desensitization, crate training, and providing them with engaging toys can assist in managing separation anxiety.

- *STUBBORNNESS:*

  Lakeland Terriers can be independent and stubborn at times. This may make training more challenging, as they may be less inclined to comply with commands. Patient and consistent training methods, using positive reinforcement, can help overcome this issue.

- *AGGRESSION:*

Although not common, some Lakeland Terriers may display aggression towards other dogs or animals, especially those of the same sex. Early socialization, proper training, and closely monitoring their interactions can help address and manage any aggressive tendencies.

- *CHASING INSTINCT:*

Due to their hunting background, Lakeland Terriers may have a strong chasing instinct towards small animals. This can be a challenge when encountering squirrels, birds, or other small pets. Training, proper leash control, and managing their environment can help minimize this behavior.

It's important to note that not all Lakeland Terriers will exhibit these behavioral issues, and individual personalities can vary. Early socialization, consistent training, and providing them with appropriate outlets for their energy and instincts can greatly contribute to a well-behaved and balanced Lakeland Terrier.

LAKELAND TERRIER

GROOMING REQUIREMENTS

The Lakeland Terrier has specific grooming requirements to maintain its distinctive coat and overall appearance. Here are some important considerations:

- *COAT MAINTENANCE:*

  The Lakeland Terrier has a double coat consisting of a harsh, wiry outer coat and a dense, soft undercoat. Regular grooming is necessary to keep the coat in good condition. Hand-stripping, a process of removing dead hair by hand, is the preferred method for maintaining the coat's texture and color. This should be done every few months, or as needed, to encourage new hair growth and prevent the coat from becoming too long or matted.

- *BRUSHING:*

  In addition to hand-stripping, regular brushing helps remove loose hair and prevent matting. Use a slicker brush or a grooming tool specifically designed for wiry coats to brush through the coat and keep it free from tangles and debris. Brushing a few times a week is generally sufficient.

- *EYES AND EARS:*

  Regularly check and clean the Lakeland Terrier's eyes and ears to prevent any buildup of dirt, debris, or excess wax. Use a damp cloth or cotton ball to gently wipe the area around the eyes and clean the outer ear area. Avoid inserting anything into the ear canal.

- *TEETH AND NAILS:*

  Dental hygiene and nail care are essential. Regularly brush the dog's teeth using a dog-specific toothpaste and trim the nails when needed. Long nails can be uncomfortable for the dog and can cause issues with walking and posture.

- *BATHING:*

  Bathing frequency depends on the dog's activities and lifestyle. Generally, Lakeland Terriers require bathing every few months or when they become visibly dirty. Use a mild dog shampoo and thoroughly rinse to remove any soap residue from the coat.

- *PROFESSIONAL GROOMING:*

  Some owners choose to seek professional grooming services for their Lakeland Terriers, especially for hand-stripping. Professional groomers are skilled in maintaining the coat's texture and can provide additional grooming services as needed.

Proper and regular grooming helps keep the Lakeland Terrier's coat healthy and looking its best. It is important to start grooming routines early to familiarize the dog with the process and make it a positive experience.

LAKELAND TERRIER

FEEDING AND NUTRITION

Feeding a balanced and nutritious diet is essential to the health and well-being of a Lakeland Terrier. Here are some important considerations regarding their feeding and nutrition:

DIETARY NEEDS:

Lakeland Terriers require a high-quality dog food that meets their specific nutritional needs. It is recommended to choose a commercially prepared dog food that is formulated for small to medium-sized breeds. Look for a product that provides a balanced blend of proteins, carbohydrates, fats, vitamins, and minerals.

PORTION CONTROL:

Portion control is important to prevent overfeeding and maintain a healthy weight. The exact amount of food required can vary depending on the dog's age, size, activity level, and metabolism. It is advisable to consult with a veterinarian to determine the appropriate portion sizes for your Lakeland Terrier.

FEEDING SCHEDULE:

Establish a consistent feeding schedule for your Lakeland Terrier. Most adult dogs do well with two meals per day, while puppies may require more frequent meals. Stick to a regular routine and avoid leaving food out all day to help regulate their eating habits.

WATER AVAILABILITY:

Ensure that fresh, clean water is always available for your Lakeland Terrier. Hydration is crucial for their overall health, digestion, and well-being. Regularly check the water bowl and refill it as needed throughout the day.

DIETARY CONSIDERATIONS:

Take into account any specific dietary considerations for your Lakeland Terrier, such as allergies, sensitivities, or health conditions. If your dog has any specific dietary needs or restrictions, consult with a veterinarian to determine the most suitable diet and appropriate food choices.

MONITORING BODY CONDITION:

Regularly monitor your Lakeland Terrier's body condition to ensure they maintain a healthy weight. Adjust their portion sizes accordingly if weight gain or loss is observed. A healthy weight helps prevent *obesity-related health issues and promotes overall well-being.*

Remember to consult with a veterinarian for personalized advice and recommendations regarding the specific feeding and nutritional needs of your Lakeland Terrier.

LAKELAND TERRIER

COMMON HEALTH ISSUES

While Lakeland Terriers are generally healthy dogs, like all breeds, they may be prone to certain health issues. Here are some common health issues commonly seen in the Lakeland Terrier:

- *LENS LUXATION:*

  Lens luxation is a condition where the lens of the eye becomes displaced, leading to vision impairment or blindness. Regular eye examinations by a veterinarian can help detect and manage this condition.

- *LEGG-CALVÉ-PERTHES DISEASE:*

  Legg-Calvé-Perthes disease is a degenerative hip condition that affects the blood supply to the femoral head, causing pain and lameness. Surgical intervention may be necessary to manage this condition.

- *PATELLAR LUXATION:*

  Patellar luxation occurs when the kneecap becomes dislocated, leading to lameness and difficulty walking. In severe cases, corrective surgery may be required.

- ## *HYPOTHYROIDISM:*

  Hypothyroidism is a hormonal disorder where the thyroid gland does not produce sufficient thyroid hormones. Symptoms may include weight gain, lethargy, and skin issues. It can be managed with lifelong medication.

- ## *VON WILLEBRAND'S DISEASE:*

  Von Willebrand's disease is an inherited bleeding disorder caused by a deficiency in a blood clotting protein. Affected dogs may experience excessive bleeding or prolonged bleeding after injury or surgery.

- ## *ALLERGIES:*

  Lakeland Terriers can be prone to allergies, which may manifest as skin irritations, itching, or gastrointestinal issues. Identifying and managing the specific allergens through diet modifications or medication can help alleviate symptoms.

- ## *PROGRESSIVE RETINAL ATROPHY (PRA):*

  PRA is a degenerative eye disease that leads to progressive vision loss and eventual blindness. Regular eye exams and genetic testing can help identify carriers of PRA and manage the disease.

It is important to note that not all Lakeland Terriers will develop these health issues, and responsible breeding practices can help reduce the risk. Regular veterinary check-ups, proper nutrition, exercise, and attention to their overall well-being can contribute to a healthier and happier Lakeland Terrier.

LAKELAND TERRIER

ESSENTIAL SUPPLIES FOR OWNERS

As a Lakeland Terrier owner, there are several essential supplies you should have to ensure the comfort, safety, and well-being of your dog. Here are some important items:

FOOD AND WATER BOWLS:

Invest in sturdy, non-slip food and water bowls that are appropriate for your Lakeland Terrier's size. Stainless steel or ceramic bowls are generally recommended as they are easy to clean and maintain.

HIGH-QUALITY DOG FOOD:

Provide your Lakeland Terrier with a high-quality dog food that meets their specific nutritional needs. Consult with a veterinarian to determine the most appropriate diet for your dog's age, size, and activity level.

COLLAR AND LEASH:

A well-fitting collar and a sturdy leash are essential for walking and controlling your Lakeland Terrier. Choose a collar that is comfortable and adjustable, and a leash that is durable and appropriate for the dog's size.

IDENTIFICATION TAGS:

Ensure your Lakeland Terrier wears an identification tag with your contact information. This is crucial in case your dog ever becomes lost. Consider including your phone number, address, and the dog's name on the tag.

DOG BED OR CRATE:

Provide your Lakeland Terrier with a comfortable and cozy dog bed or crate where they can rest and feel secure. Choose a size appropriate for your dog to allow them to stretch out and relax.

GROOMING TOOLS:

Invest in grooming tools specifically designed for a Lakeland Terrier's coat, such as a slicker brush, stripping knife, and comb. These tools will help you maintain the coat's texture and keep it free from tangles.

TOYS AND ENRICHMENT:

Provide your Lakeland Terrier with a variety of toys for mental stimulation and entertainment. Interactive toys, chew toys, and puzzle toys can help keep them occupied and prevent boredom.

DOG CRATE OR GATE:

A dog crate or gate can be useful for creating a safe space for your Lakeland Terrier or for restricting their access to certain areas of the house. It can also aid in housetraining and keeping them secure when necessary.

DOG SHAMPOO AND GROOMING PRODUCTS:

Have dog-specific shampoo and grooming products on hand for bathing and maintaining your Lakeland Terrier's coat and hygiene. Use products that are safe and appropriate for their coat type.

FIRST AID KIT:

Keep a basic first aid kit for your Lakeland Terrier, including items such as bandages, antiseptic solution, styptic powder, and any medications prescribed by your veterinarian.

These essential supplies will help you provide a comfortable and fulfilling life for your Lakeland Terrier while meeting their basic needs. Remember to regularly inspect and replace items as needed to ensure the safety and well-being of your beloved companion.

CREATING A SAFE AND COMFORTABLE ENVIRONMENT

Creating a safe and comfortable environment is crucial for the well-being of your Lakeland Terrier. Here are some important considerations to ensure their safety and comfort:

SECURE LIVING SPACE:

Ensure that your living space is secure and free from hazards. Close off areas that may be dangerous or inaccessible for your Lakeland Terrier, such as staircases or rooms with potential hazards. Use gates or crates to restrict access when necessary.

INDOOR SAFETY:

Remove toxic plants, chemicals, and hazardous substances from your Lakeland Terrier's reach. Keep small objects, electrical cords, and potentially dangerous items out of their reach to prevent ingestion or accidents. Use childproof locks on cabinets if needed.

OUTDOOR SAFETY:

When allowing your Lakeland Terrier outside, ensure that your yard is securely fenced to prevent them from wandering off. Regularly inspect the fencing for any gaps or loose sections. Create a designated area for them to play and explore, and supervise them to prevent them from escaping or encountering potential dangers.

COMFORTABLE RESTING SPACE:

Provide a comfortable resting space for your Lakeland Terrier, such as a soft dog bed or crate. Make sure the bed is appropriately sized and placed in a quiet and cozy area where they can relax and feel secure.

TEMPERATURE CONTROL:

Maintain a comfortable temperature within your home. Ensure that your Lakeland Terrier has access to a cool area during hot weather and a warm area during colder seasons. Avoid leaving them in extreme temperatures, whether indoors or outdoors.

APPROPRIATE EXERCISE AND STIMULATION:

Provide regular exercise and mental stimulation for your Lakeland Terrier. Engage in daily walks, play sessions, and interactive toys to keep them physically and mentally stimulated. This helps prevent boredom and destructive behaviors.

SOCIALIZATION AND TRAINING:

Socialize your Lakeland Terrier from a young age, exposing them to various people, animals, and environments. Proper training and positive reinforcement techniques will help them become well-behaved and responsive companions.

VETERINARY CARE:

Ensure regular veterinary check-ups, vaccinations, and preventive treatments for your Lakeland Terrier. Follow your veterinarian's recommendations for vaccinations, parasite control, and general health care to keep your dog healthy and protected.

By creating a safe and comfortable environment, you can provide your Lakeland Terrier with a happy and fulfilling life, promoting their overall well-being and ensuring their safety at all times.

LAKELAND TERRIER

HEALTH CONCERNS AND COMMON MEDICAL ISSUES

The Lakeland Terrier is generally a healthy breed, but like all dogs, they may be prone to certain health concerns and medical issues. Here are some common health concerns seen in Lakeland Terriers:

LENS LUXATION:

Lens luxation is a condition where the lens of the eye becomes displaced, leading to vision impairment or blindness. Regular eye examinations can help detect and manage this condition.

LEGG-CALVÉ-PERTHES DISEASE:

Legg-Calvé-Perthes disease is a degenerative hip condition that affects the blood supply to the femoral head, causing pain and lameness. Surgical intervention may be necessary to manage this condition.

PATELLAR LUXATION:

Patellar luxation occurs when the kneecap becomes dislocated, leading to lameness and difficulty walking. In severe cases, corrective surgery may be required.

HYPOTHYROIDISM:

Hypothyroidism is a hormonal disorder where the thyroid gland does not produce sufficient thyroid hormones. Symptoms may include weight gain, lethargy, and skin issues. It can be managed with lifelong medication.

VON WILLEBRAND'S DISEASE:

Von Willebrand's disease is an inherited bleeding disorder caused by a deficiency in a blood clotting protein. Affected dogs may experience excessive bleeding or prolonged bleeding after injury or surgery.

ALLERGIES:

Lakeland Terriers can be prone to allergies, which may manifest as skin irritations, itching, or gastrointestinal issues. Identifying and managing the specific allergens through diet modifications or medication can help alleviate symptoms.

PROGRESSIVE RETINAL ATROPHY (PRA):

PRA is a degenerative eye disease that leads to progressive vision loss and eventual blindness. Regular eye exams and genetic testing can help identify carriers of PRA and manage the disease.

It's important to note that not all Lakeland Terriers will develop these health issues, and responsible breeding practices can help reduce the risk. Regular veterinary check-ups, maintaining a healthy diet, providing appropriate exercise, and attending to their overall well-being can contribute to a healthier and happier Lakeland Terrier.

LAKELAND TERRIER

REGULAR HEALTH CHECK-UPS AND VACCINATIONS

Regular health check-ups and vaccinations are essential for maintaining the health and well-being of your Lakeland Terrier. Here are some important considerations:

HEALTH CHECK-UPS:

Schedule regular veterinary check-ups for your Lakeland Terrier, usually once or twice a year. During these check-ups, the veterinarian will perform a comprehensive examination to assess your dog's overall health, identify any potential health issues, and provide appropriate recommendations.

VACCINATIONS:

Vaccinations are crucial for preventing various infectious diseases that can affect your Lakeland Terrier's health. Common vaccinations for dogs include:

- RABIES:

Rabies vaccination is essential for protecting your dog against this deadly viral disease. Rabies vaccinations are typically required by law in many regions.

- *DISTEMPER:*

Distemper is a highly contagious viral disease that affects the respiratory, gastrointestinal, and nervous systems. Vaccination helps protect your dog from this serious illness.

- *HEPATITIS:*

Canine hepatitis is a viral infection that affects the liver and can lead to severe illness. Vaccination against hepatitis is an important preventive measure.

- *PARVOVIRUS:*

Parvovirus is a highly contagious and potentially fatal disease that affects the gastrointestinal tract. Vaccination provides protection against this serious viral infection.

- *PARAINFLUENZA:*

Parainfluenza is a respiratory virus commonly associated with canine cough (kennel cough). Vaccination helps reduce the risk and severity of this respiratory illness.

- *LEPTOSPIROSIS:*

  Leptospirosis is a bacterial infection that can cause serious kidney and liver damage. Vaccination is recommended for dogs at risk of exposure to this disease.

ADDITIONAL PREVENTIVE MEASURES:

Aside from vaccinations, your veterinarian may recommend additional preventive measures for your Lakeland Terrier, such as regular parasite control (fleas, ticks, and worms), heartworm prevention, and dental care. Follow your veterinarian's advice regarding these preventive measures to ensure your dog's optimal health.

Remember to maintain a record of your Lakeland Terrier's vaccinations and keep it up to date. This will help ensure that your dog is protected against preventable diseases and promote their overall well-being.

ALLERGIES: COMMON TRIGGERS AND MANAGEMENT

Lakeland Terriers, like many other dog breeds, can be prone to allergies. Allergies occur when the immune system overreacts to certain substances, triggering a range of symptoms. Here's some information on common triggers and management of allergies in Lakeland Terriers:

COMMON ALLERGY TRIGGERS:

1.

ENVIRONMENTAL ALLERGENS:

Environmental allergens such as pollen, mold spores, dust mites, and certain plants can trigger allergies in Lakeland Terriers. These allergens are often inhaled and can cause respiratory symptoms and skin reactions.

2.

FLEAS AND PARASITES:

Flea bites can cause allergic reactions in dogs, leading to itching, skin irritation, and discomfort. Other parasites, such as mites, can also trigger allergic responses.

3.

FOOD ALLERGENS:

Certain ingredients in dog food, such as beef, chicken, dairy, wheat, or soy, can cause food allergies in Lakeland Terriers. These allergies often result in skin problems, gastrointestinal issues, or ear infections.

MANAGING ALLERGIES:

1.

IDENTIFYING AND AVOIDING TRIGGERS:

Work with your veterinarian to identify the specific allergens triggering your Lakeland Terrier's allergies. Once identified, take steps to reduce exposure to these allergens. For example, keep your dog indoors during peak pollen seasons and regularly clean their living environment to minimize dust and mold.

2.

REGULAR BATHING:

Frequent bathing can help alleviate allergy symptoms by removing allergens from your dog's coat and skin. Use a hypoallergenic dog shampoo recommended by your veterinarian and follow proper bathing techniques.

3.

MEDICATIONS AND TREATMENTS:

Your veterinarian may prescribe medications or treatments to manage your Lakeland Terrier's allergies. These may include antihistamines, corticosteroids, or immune-modulating drugs to control symptoms and reduce the immune system's overreactivity.

4.

DIETARY MODIFICATIONS:

If food allergies are suspected, your veterinarian may recommend an elimination diet or a hypoallergenic diet trial to identify and eliminate problem ingredients. Feeding a balanced, high-quality diet tailored to your dog's specific needs can help support their overall health and manage allergic reactions.

5.

REGULAR VETERINARY CARE:

Regular veterinary check-ups are essential for monitoring your Lakeland Terrier's allergies and adjusting the treatment plan as needed. Your veterinarian can also address any secondary infections or complications that may arise due to allergies.

It's important to work closely with your veterinarian to develop an individualized allergy management plan for your Lakeland Terrier. With proper care and management, you can help minimize your dog's exposure to allergens and provide relief from allergy symptoms, improving their quality of life.

LAKELAND TERRIER

TRAVEL ESSENTIALS: WHAT TO PACK FOR A TRIP

When planning a trip with your Lakeland Terrier, it's important to pack the necessary essentials to ensure their comfort, safety, and well-being. Here are some travel essentials to consider:

FOOD AND WATER:

Pack enough of your Lakeland Terrier's regular dog food to last the duration of the trip. It's also essential to bring portable food and water bowls for feeding and hydration on the go. Make sure to have access to clean drinking water during your travels.

LEASH AND COLLAR:

Bring a sturdy leash and a properly fitting collar or harness for your Lakeland Terrier. These items are essential for walking and ensuring your dog's safety in unfamiliar surroundings. Consider using a reflective collar or leash for added visibility during nighttime walks.

IDENTIFICATION AND TRAVEL DOCUMENTS:

Carry identification tags with your contact information and ensure your Lakeland Terrier is microchipped with updated registration. Additionally, bring any necessary travel documents, such as vaccination records, health certificates, and identification papers required by your destination or mode of travel.

COMFORTABLE BEDDING:

Provide your Lakeland Terrier with familiar and comfortable bedding for resting during the trip. This can be a portable dog bed, blanket, or crate pad that they are accustomed to using. Having a familiar sleeping area will help them feel more secure and relaxed.

MEDICATIONS AND FIRST AID KIT:

If your Lakeland Terrier requires any medications, ensure you have an ample supply for the duration of the trip. Pack a pet-specific first aid kit that includes basic supplies like bandages, antiseptic solution, tweezers, and any necessary medications prescribed by your veterinarian.

TOYS AND ENTERTAINMENT:

Bring your Lakeland Terrier's favorite toys, chew items, or interactive puzzles to keep them entertained during travel and downtime. Familiar toys can provide comfort and help alleviate stress or boredom during the journey.

CLEANING SUPPLIES:

Pack cleaning supplies such as poop bags, paper towels, wet wipes, or pet-safe disinfectant. These items will help you maintain cleanliness and hygiene during the trip, especially when dealing with accidents or messes.

TRAVEL CRATE OR SAFETY RESTRAINT:

If traveling by car, consider using a travel crate or a safety restraint system to secure your Lakeland Terrier during the journey. This helps ensure their safety and prevents distractions for the driver. Familiarize your dog with the crate or restraint system before the trip to make them more comfortable.

Remember to research and plan your trip in advance, considering your Lakeland Terrier's specific needs and any regulations or restrictions at your destination. By packing these travel essentials, you can help ensure a smooth and enjoyable trip for both you and your beloved Lakeland Terrier.

LAKELAND TERRIER

APPROPRIATE TOYS AND ENRICHMENT ACTIVITIES

Providing appropriate toys and enrichment activities is essential for keeping your Lakeland Terrier mentally stimulated and engaged. Here are some options to consider:

INTERACTIVE PUZZLE TOYS:

Interactive puzzle toys challenge your Lakeland Terrier's problem-solving skills and keep them mentally stimulated. These toys typically involve hiding treats or kibble inside compartments or requiring your dog to solve a puzzle to access the reward.

CHEW TOYS:

Chew toys are important for satisfying your Lakeland Terrier's natural urge to chew and promoting dental health. Look for durable chew toys made from safe materials, such as rubber or nylon, that are designed for moderate to heavy chewers.

PLUSH TOYS:

Plush toys can provide comfort and serve as cuddle buddies for your Lakeland Terrier. Look for well-made plush toys without small parts that can be easily chewed off and ingested. Rotate plush toys to keep them interesting and avoid excessive wear and tear.

TUG TOYS:

Tug toys are great for interactive play and bonding with your Lakeland Terrier. Look for sturdy tug toys made from durable materials, such as rope or rubber, that can withstand the pulling and tugging during play sessions.

SQUEAKY TOYS:

Squeaky toys can engage your Lakeland Terrier's natural hunting instincts and provide auditory stimulation. Opt for high-quality squeaky toys that are designed to withstand moderate chewing and have secure squeakers to prevent accidental ingestion.

FETCH TOYS:

Fetch toys, such as balls or flying discs, are great for outdoor play and exercise. Choose toys that are appropriately sized for your Lakeland Terrier and made from safe materials that won't harm their teeth or gums.

TRAINING TOYS:

Training toys, such as treat-dispensing toys or clicker training kits, can be used to engage your Lakeland Terrier's mind while teaching them new commands and tricks. These toys can provide mental stimulation while reinforcing positive behaviors.

ROTATING TOYS:

Rotate your Lakeland Terrier's toys regularly to keep them fresh and interesting. This prevents boredom and ensures that your dog remains engaged and excited about their toys. Keep a variety of toys available and switch them out periodically.

Always supervise your Lakeland Terrier while playing with toys to ensure their safety. Remove any damaged or worn-out toys to prevent choking hazards. Remember that each dog may have different preferences, so observe your Lakeland Terrier's behavior to determine which toys and activities they enjoy the most.

LAKELAND TERRIER

INTELLIGENCE AND TRAINABILITY

Lakeland Terriers are intelligent and trainable dogs. Here's some information about their intelligence and trainability:

INTELLIGENCE:

Lakeland Terriers are known for their intelligence. They have a quick and alert mind, which makes them responsive to training and adaptable to different situations. Their intelligence allows them to learn new commands and tasks relatively quickly.

TRAINABILITY:

Lakeland Terriers are generally trainable, but they can have an independent and stubborn streak at times. They require consistent, positive reinforcement-based training methods that focus on rewards, praise, and motivation. Harsh or forceful training techniques are not recommended for this breed, as it can lead to resistance and mistrust.

SOCIALIZATION:

Proper socialization is important for Lakeland Terriers. Early and ongoing socialization with various people, animals, and environments helps them develop into well-rounded and confident dogs. Exposing them to different situations and positive experiences helps prevent fear or aggression towards new stimuli.

OBEDIENCE TRAINING:

Basic obedience training is essential for Lakeland Terriers. Start training from a young age, focusing on commands such as sit, stay, come, and leash walking. Use positive reinforcement techniques, reward-based training, and short, engaging training sessions to keep their attention and motivation high.

TASK TRAINING:

Lakeland Terriers have the potential to excel in various tasks and activities beyond basic obedience. They can participate in agility, rally, obedience trials, and even canine sports like scent work or tracking. Their intelligence and agility make them well-suited for these activities.

MENTAL STIMULATION:

Providing mental stimulation is crucial for the well-being of Lakeland Terriers. Engage them in interactive games, puzzle toys, and training sessions to keep their minds active and prevent boredom. Mental stimulation helps prevent destructive behaviors that can arise from excess energy or lack of mental engagement.

Remember that every dog is unique, and individual temperament and personality can vary. Some Lakeland Terriers may be more eager to please and trainable, while others may require more patience and persistence. With consistent training, positive reinforcement, and patience, you can shape your Lakeland Terrier into a well-behaved and obedient companion.

TRAINING TECHNIQUES

When it comes to training a Lakeland Terrier, positive reinforcement-based techniques are highly recommended. Here are some training techniques that work well for this breed:

1. POSITIVE REINFORCEMENT:

Positive reinforcement involves rewarding desired behaviors to encourage their repetition. Use treats, praise, and affection as rewards when your Lakeland Terrier follows commands correctly or exhibits good behavior. This approach helps build a strong bond between you and your dog and motivates them to learn and please you.

2. CONSISTENCY:

Consistency is key when training a Lakeland Terrier. Use consistent commands and signals for each behavior you want to teach. This helps your dog understand and respond more effectively. Consistency should also apply to the rules and boundaries you establish, ensuring that everyone in the household follows the same guidelines.

3. SHORT AND ENGAGING TRAINING SESSIONS:

Lakeland Terriers have relatively short attention spans, so keep training sessions brief and engaging. Aim for multiple short sessions throughout the day rather than one long session. This helps maintain your dog's focus and prevents them from becoming bored or overwhelmed.

4. PATIENCE AND POSITIVE ATTITUDE:

Patience is essential during training. Avoid getting frustrated or losing your temper if your Lakeland Terrier doesn't grasp a command immediately. Stay calm and maintain a positive attitude. Dogs respond best to positive reinforcement and encouragement, so celebrate small successes along the way.

5. SOCIALIZATION:

Socialization is crucial for Lakeland Terriers to become well-rounded and confident dogs. Expose them to different environments, people, animals, and situations from a young age. This helps them learn to adapt and be comfortable in various settings, reducing the likelihood of fear or aggression towards new stimuli.

6. TRAINING FOR REAL-LIFE SITUATIONS:

While teaching basic obedience commands is important, also focus on training your Lakeland Terrier for real-life situations. Practice commands like "stay," "come," and "leave it" in various environments with distractions. This prepares your dog to respond reliably in different scenarios and enhances their overall training effectiveness.

7. PROFESSIONAL TRAINING CLASSES:

Consider enrolling your Lakeland Terrier in professional training classes or working with a certified dog trainer. These classes provide structured training environments, expert guidance, and opportunities for socialization with other dogs. Professional trainers can offer personalized advice and address specific training challenges you may encounter.

Remember, training should always be a positive and enjoyable experience for both you and your Lakeland Terrier. By using positive reinforcement techniques, being consistent, and providing appropriate socialization, you can help your dog become well-behaved, obedient, and a loving companion.

LAKELAND TERRIER

BENEFITS OF REGULAR EXERCISE AND MENTAL STIMULATION

Regular exercise and mental stimulation are vital for the overall well-being of a Lakeland Terrier. Here are some benefits of providing them with both physical and mental stimulation:

1. PHYSICAL FITNESS:

Regular exercise *helps keep your Lakeland Terrier physically fit and maintains a healthy weight. Engaging in activities such as brisk walks, jogging, or play sessions helps strengthen their muscles, improves cardiovascular health, and promotes overall physical endurance.*

2. MENTAL STIMULATION:

Mental stimulation *is essential for preventing boredom and keeping your Lakeland Terrier's mind sharp. Engaging them in activities that challenge their problem-solving skills and require them to think and make decisions helps stimulate their cognitive abilities.*

3. ENERGY RELEASE:

Providing regular exercise helps **release excess energy** in Lakeland Terriers. This breed has a moderate energy level and requires daily exercise to prevent restlessness and potential destructive behaviors that can arise from pent-up energy.

4. BEHAVIOR MANAGEMENT:

Regular exercise and mental stimulation contribute to **behavior management.** A well-exercised and mentally stimulated Lakeland Terrier is less likely to engage in destructive chewing, excessive barking, or other undesirable behaviors that may arise from boredom or lack of stimulation.

5. BONDING AND SOCIALIZATION:

Engaging in activities with your Lakeland Terrier strengthens the **bond** between you and your dog. Whether it's going for walks, playing fetch, or participating in training sessions, these shared experiences enhance your relationship and build trust. Additionally, exercise and socialization opportunities can help your dog become well-socialized and comfortable around people, other animals, and different environments.

6. STRESS REDUCTION:

Regular exercise and mental stimulation are excellent outlets for **reducing stress** in Lakeland Terriers. Physical activity releases endorphins, which promote feelings of well-being and help alleviate stress and anxiety. Mental stimulation activities provide mental relaxation and prevent boredom-related stress.

7. OVERALL HEALTH AND LONGEVITY:

By providing regular exercise and mental stimulation, you are contributing to your Lakeland Terrier's **overall health** and **longevity**. Regular physical activity helps maintain a healthy weight, strengthens their immune system, and improves their overall physical and mental well-being.

Remember to tailor the exercise and mental stimulation activities to your Lakeland Terrier's individual needs and abilities. Consult with your veterinarian to determine the appropriate amount and type of exercise for your dog's age, health condition, and energy level. By incorporating regular exercise and mental stimulation into your Lakeland Terrier's routine, you can ensure they lead a happy, fulfilled, and healthy life.

BREEDING AND RESPONSIBLE OWNERSHIP

Breeding and responsible ownership are crucial considerations when it comes to maintaining the health and well-being of the Lakeland Terrier breed. Here are some important aspects to keep in mind:

1. RESPONSIBLE BREEDING:

Breeding *should be done responsibly and with the goal of improving the breed. Responsible breeders prioritize the health, temperament, and conformation of the dogs. They conduct health tests, screen for genetic disorders, and select breeding pairs carefully to minimize the risk of inherited health issues.*

2. HEALTH TESTING:

Responsible breeders **perform health tests** *on their breeding dogs to ensure they are free from known hereditary conditions. Common health tests for Lakeland Terriers include eye examinations, hip evaluations, and genetic tests for specific disorders. These tests help identify potential health risks and allow breeders to make informed decisions when selecting mating pairs.*

3. ETHICAL PRACTICES:

Responsible breeders adhere to **ethical practices** that prioritize the well-being of their dogs. This includes providing proper veterinary care, nutrition, exercise, and socialization. They also ensure that their dogs have suitable living conditions and are treated with love, care, and respect.

4. BREED STANDARDS:

Responsible breeders strive to **maintain and improve** the breed according to the established breed standards. They have a deep understanding of the breed's characteristics, including physical traits, temperament, and working abilities. By breeding to the standard, they aim to preserve the breed's integrity and ensure that future generations exhibit the desired breed traits.

5. EDUCATION AND SUPPORT:

Responsible breeders **educate** potential owners about the breed's characteristics, requirements, and potential challenges. They provide ongoing support and guidance to new puppy owners, offering advice on health care, training, socialization, and responsible ownership practices. They are committed to the lifelong well-being of the puppies they breed.

6. RESPONSIBLE OWNERSHIP:

As an owner of a Lakeland Terrier, it is your responsibility to **provide** proper care, training, socialization, and a loving home. This includes providing a balanced diet, regular veterinary care, exercise, mental stimulation, and a safe environment. Responsible owners also comply with local laws and regulations, such as licensing and vaccination requirements.

7. ADOPTION AND RESCUE:

Another option for acquiring a Lakeland Terrier is through **adoption or rescue** organizations. Many wonderful dogs are in need of loving homes, and adopting a rescued Lakeland Terrier can be a rewarding experience. These organizations often conduct thorough assessments of the dogs' health and temperament to ensure compatibility with potential adopters.

By prioritizing responsible breeding practices and being a responsible owner, you contribute to the overall well-being and preservation of the Lakeland Terrier breed. Responsible ownership ensures that these wonderful dogs can live happy, healthy lives and thrive as beloved companions.

NEUTERING/SPAYING: BENEFITS AND CONSIDERATIONS

Neutering (for males) and spaying (for females) are common procedures performed on dogs, including the Lakeland Terrier breed. Here are some benefits and considerations to keep in mind:

BENEFITS OF NEUTERING/SPAYING:

1. Population Control: *One of the primary benefits of neutering/spaying is to help control the population of dogs. By preventing unwanted litters, you contribute to reducing the number of dogs in shelters and the incidence of stray and abandoned dogs.*

2. Prevention of Reproductive Health Issues: *Neutering male Lakeland Terriers can help prevent testicular cancer, reduce the risk of prostate problems, and eliminate the risk of certain reproductive-related conditions. Spaying female Lakeland Terriers can prevent uterine infections (such as pyometra) and reduce the risk of mammary tumors, especially if done before their first heat cycle.*

3. Behavioral Benefits: *Neutering/spaying can have positive effects on behavior. It can help reduce or* eliminate certain unwanted behaviors, such as roaming, marking territory with urine, aggression related to mating instincts, and the attraction of intact dogs during the female's heat cycle.

CONSIDERATIONS:

1. Timing: *The timing of neutering/spaying is an important consideration. It is generally recommended to wait until the dog reaches sexual maturity and completes most of their physical growth. Consult with your veterinarian to determine the most appropriate timing for your Lakeland Terrier.*

2. Health and Individual Needs: *Consider the health and individual needs of your Lakeland Terrier when deciding on neutering/spaying. Discuss with your veterinarian to weigh the potential health benefits against any breed-specific considerations or individual health concerns that may influence the decision.*

3. Potential Weight Management:
Neutering/spaying can slightly alter the metabolism and hormone levels of dogs, which may affect their tendency to gain weight. It's important to monitor your Lakeland Terrier's diet and exercise routine to prevent excessive weight gain and maintain a healthy body condition.

4. Responsible Ownership: *Whether you choose to neuter/spay your Lakeland Terrier or not, responsible ownership includes taking measures to prevent accidental breeding and ensuring the safety and well-being of your dog and any potential offspring.*

Consult with your veterinarian to discuss the benefits and considerations specific to your Lakeland Terrier. They can provide personalized advice and guidance based on your dog's health, age, and individual circumstances.

LAKELAND TERRIER

LIFESPAN AND AGING PROCESS

The lifespan and aging process of a Lakeland Terrier are influenced by various factors, including genetics, overall health, diet, and lifestyle. Here's some information about their typical lifespan and aging process:

LIFESPAN:

The average **lifespan** of a Lakeland Terrier is around 12 to 15 years. However, with proper care and a healthy lifestyle, some individuals may live even longer.

AGING PROCESS:

Like all living beings, Lakeland Terriers undergo an **aging process** as they grow older. Here are some common changes that may occur:

1. PHYSICAL CHANGES:

As Lakeland Terriers age, they may experience a decline in physical abilities. Their energy levels may decrease, and they may become less active. They may also develop gray hair, experience a loss of muscle mass, and show signs of joint stiffness or arthritis.

2. COGNITIVE CHANGES:

Senior Lakeland Terriers may undergo **cognitive changes** as they age. They may become less responsive to commands, have difficulty learning new tasks, or show signs of memory loss. Some dogs may develop age-related cognitive decline, also known as canine cognitive dysfunction, which can lead to disorientation and changes in behavior.

3. HEALTH ISSUES:

As Lakeland Terriers age, they may become more prone to certain **health issues** associated with aging. These can include arthritis, dental problems, vision or hearing loss, heart disease, and metabolic disorders. Regular veterinary check-ups, preventive care, and a balanced diet can help manage and address these age-related health concerns.

4. LIFESTYLE ADJUSTMENTS:

To accommodate the aging process, **lifestyle adjustments** may be necessary. Providing a comfortable and safe environment becomes crucial, ensuring easy access to their bed, food, and water. Regular exercise is still important, but it may need to *be modified to accommodate their physical abilities and limitations.*

5. SENIOR CARE:

*As Lakeland Terriers enter their senior years, they benefit from **specialized senior care**. This may involve regular veterinary check-ups, senior-specific diets, joint supplements, and modifications to their exercise routine. Monitoring their health closely and addressing any age-related issues promptly can help maintain their quality of life.*

Remember, individual Lakeland Terriers may age differently based on various factors. Paying attention to their specific needs and providing appropriate care can help them age gracefully and enjoy their senior years to the fullest.

DEALING WITH SEASONAL CHANGES AND EXTREME TEMPERATURES

Seasonal changes and extreme temperatures can have an impact on the well-being of a Lakeland Terrier. Here are some considerations for dealing with these conditions:

ADAPTING TO SEASONAL CHANGES:

As seasons change, it's important to take certain measures to ensure your Lakeland Terrier's comfort and safety:

1. EXTREME HEAT:

During hot weather:

- Avoid walking or exercising your Lakeland Terrier during the hottest parts of the day when temperatures are high.
- Provide access to shade and plenty of fresh water to prevent dehydration.
- Avoid leaving your dog in a parked car, as temperatures can rise dangerously within minutes.
- Consider using cooling mats, bandanas, or portable fans to help keep your dog cool.

2. EXTREME COLD:

During cold weather:

- Limit your Lakeland Terrier's exposure to extreme cold and inclement weather, such as heavy rain, snow, or strong winds.
- Consider using doggy jackets or sweaters to provide extra warmth during chilly temperatures.
- Keep walks and outdoor activities shorter in very cold weather to avoid overexposure.
- Wipe your dog's paws after walks to remove any ice or snow and to prevent irritation or frostbite.

GENERAL TIPS:

Regardless of the season, here are some general tips for dealing with temperature changes:

- Monitor your Lakeland Terrier's behavior and watch for signs of discomfort or distress, such as excessive panting, shivering, or seeking shelter.
- Provide a comfortable indoor environment with appropriate heating or cooling systems to keep your dog comfortable.
- Adjust exercise routines and intensity to suit the temperature and your dog's individual needs.
- Consult with your veterinarian for specific recommendations on managing extreme temperatures and seasonal changes.

Remember, every dog is different, and their tolerance to temperature changes may vary. It's important to observe your Lakeland Terrier's behavior and make adjustments accordingly to ensure their well-being during seasonal transitions and extreme weather conditions.

LAKELAND TERRIER

TYPES OF BREED STANDARDS

There are different types of breed standards for the Lakeland Terrier, which serve as guidelines for the ideal characteristics and appearance of the breed. These standards are established by kennel clubs and breed organizations. Here are the main types of breed standards:

1. AMERICAN KENNEL CLUB (AKC) STANDARD:

The **American Kennel Club (AKC)** sets the breed standard for Lakeland Terriers in the United States. The AKC standard outlines the desired physical attributes, temperament, and overall appearance of the breed, including details such as size, coat color and texture, head shape, ear placement, and tail carriage.

2. THE KENNEL CLUB (UK) STANDARD:

The **The Kennel Club (UK)** is the governing body for dog breeds in the United Kingdom. They have their own breed standard for the Lakeland Terrier, which outlines the desired characteristics specific to the breed. The UK standard may have slight differences compared to other standards in terms of preferred traits or conformation details.

3. FÉDÉRATION CYNOLOGIQUE INTERNATIONALE (FCI) STANDARD:

The **Fédération Cynologique Internationale (FCI)** is an international federation of kennel clubs that sets breed standards for various dog breeds, including the Lakeland Terrier. The FCI standard provides guidelines for breeders, judges, and enthusiasts around the world regarding the ideal conformation and characteristics of the breed.

While the overall goals and characteristics are generally consistent across these different standards, minor variations in wording or emphasis may exist. It's important to refer to the specific breed standard recognized by the kennel club or organization in your country or region for detailed guidelines on the Lakeland Terrier's conformation and breed traits.

These breed standards help maintain breed consistency and serve as a reference for breeders, judges, and enthusiasts to evaluate and assess Lakeland Terriers in conformation shows and breeding programs.

LAKELAND TERRIER

MYTHS AND MISCONCEPTIONS DEBUNKED

There are several myths and misconceptions surrounding the Lakeland Terrier breed. Let's debunk some of these misconceptions:

1. MYTH: LAKELAND TERRIERS ARE AGGRESSIVE.

*The truth is that **Lakeland Terriers are not inherently aggressive**. Like any breed, their behavior is influenced by factors such as socialization, training, and individual temperament. With proper socialization and training, Lakeland Terriers can be friendly, well-behaved, and sociable dogs.*

2. MYTH: LAKELAND TERRIERS ARE HIGH-MAINTENANCE AND DIFFICULT TO GROOM.

While Lakeland Terriers have a distinctive, wiry coat, it does not necessarily mean they are excessively high-maintenance. Regular brushing, occasional hand-stripping, and professional grooming can help maintain their coat. With proper grooming techniques and regular care, grooming a Lakeland Terrier can be manageable and enjoyable.

3. MYTH: LAKELAND TERRIERS ARE NOT GOOD WITH CHILDREN.

The truth is that **Lakeland Terriers can be excellent family dogs** and get along well with children when properly socialized and trained. Like any dog breed, it's important to supervise interactions between dogs and children to ensure mutual respect and safety.

4. MYTH: LAKELAND TERRIERS REQUIRE A LARGE LIVING SPACE AND CANNOT ADAPT TO APARTMENT LIVING.

Lakeland Terriers are adaptable and can adjust well to different living situations, including apartment living. While they do require regular exercise and mental stimulation, they can thrive in smaller spaces as long as their exercise needs are met through daily walks, play sessions, and interactive activities.

5. MYTH: LAKELAND TERRIERS ARE NOT SUITABLE FOR FIRST-TIME DOG OWNERS.

While Lakeland Terriers can be independent and strong-willed at times, they can still be suitable for first-time dog owners who are committed to providing proper training, socialization, and care. With patience, consistency, and positive reinforcement-based training methods, first-time owners can successfully raise and enjoy a Lakeland Terrier.

6. MYTH: ALL LAKELAND TERRIERS ARE GOOD WITH OTHER SMALL PETS.

While Lakeland Terriers can generally coexist with other pets, their compatibility may vary depending on the individual dog's temperament and early socialization experiences. Some Lakeland Terriers may have a higher prey drive and may need careful introductions and supervision when interacting with smaller animals.

It's important to separate fact from fiction when it comes to breed-specific traits and behaviors. Every dog, including the Lakeland Terrier, is an individual with their own personality and tendencies. Responsible ownership, proper training, socialization, and understanding the needs of the breed are key to fostering a happy and well-adjusted Lakeland Terrier.

CONCLUSION

The Lakeland Terrier is a delightful breed known for its spunky personality, intelligence, and distinctive wiry coat. With their sturdy build and playful nature, they make excellent companions for individuals and families alike. Here are some key points to remember about this breed:

1. UNIQUE CHARACTERISTICS:

The Lakeland Terrier is a small to medium-sized breed with a charming appearance and expressive eyes. Their dense, double-layered coat requires regular grooming and hand-stripping to maintain its characteristic texture. They come in various color variations, including black, blue, liver, and wheaten.

2. TEMPERAMENT AND PERSONALITY:

Lakeland Terriers are known for their confidence, intelligence, and spirited nature. They are friendly, loyal, and often exhibit a sense of humor. They can be independent at times, but with proper training and socialization, they can be well-mannered and sociable companions.

3. EXERCISE AND MENTAL STIMULATION:

Lakeland Terriers require regular exercise to keep them physically and mentally stimulated. Daily walks, interactive play sessions, and engaging activities help fulfill their energy needs and prevent behavioral issues that may arise from boredom or lack of stimulation.

4. TRAINING AND SOCIALIZATION:

Positive reinforcement-based training techniques are effective for Lakeland Terriers. Consistency, patience, and early socialization are crucial in shaping them into well-behaved and confident dogs. They can excel in various training activities, sports, and tasks beyond basic obedience.

5. HEALTH AND CARE:

Lakeland Terriers are generally healthy dogs, but they may be prone to certain health issues such as patellar luxation, lens luxation, and autoimmune disorders. Regular veterinary check-ups, a balanced diet, proper grooming, and preventive care help ensure their well-being.

The Lakeland Terrier's charming personality, intelligence, and adaptability make them a wonderful choice for individuals or families seeking a lively and loyal companion. With responsible ownership, proper training, and the love and care they deserve, Lakeland Terriers can bring joy and companionship to their owners for many years to come.

Printed in Great Britain
by Amazon

27207663R00056